CATERPILLAR

GREAT AMERICAN LEGEND

Photography by Henry Rasmussen

Motorbooks International
Publishers & Wholesalers Inc.
Osceola, Wisconsin 54020, USA   ®

CATERPILLAR

GREAT AMERICAN LEGEND

Photography by Henry Rasmussen

Motorbooks International
Publishers & Wholesalers Inc.

First published in 1986 by Motorbooks International Publishers & Wholesalers Inc, PO Box 2, 729 Prospect Avenue, Osceola, WI 54020 USA

Printed and bound in Hong Kong

The information in this book is true and complete to the best of our knowledge. All recommendations are made without any guarantee on the part of the author or publisher, who also disclaim any liability incurred in connection with the use of this data or specific details

Library of Congress Cataloging-in-Publication Data

Rasmussen, Henry
    Caterpillar, great American legend.

    1.   Caterpillar tractors. 2. Caterpillar Tractor Company--History. I. Title.
TL233.5.R37 1986   629.2'25   86-12753
ISBN 0-87938-222-8

Cover:
A D8H of late-fifties vintage, applies all of its 270 drawbar horsepower to the task of pushing a mountain of the rich black soil that inhabits the shores of the Mississippi River. Veteran Cat operator John McCarroll of Moline, Illinois, is firmly in control of his machine as it is engaged in rebuilding a levy.

Half title:
As Benjamin Holt's first track-type tractor — developed in 1904 — returned from a test run, he and a friend watched its progress. "It crawls just like a caterpillar," the friend remarked. "Caterpillar it is! That's the name for it!" Holt exclaimed. The Caterpillar name was registered in 1910. The photograph shows the logo on the radiator of a 2-Ton from the late-twenties.

Title page:
This pristine Ten belongs to Ed Porter, Salinas, California. It was bought new by a relative, and has spent all its life in the area.

Contents

The Right Tools

Man has always built on a grand scale. The Tower of Babel. The Pyramids. The Chinese Wall. The fact that he did not have much more than his hands to work with did not stop him from creating these wonders of human endeavor. But we will never know what kind of fantastic monuments would have been erected had the necessary tools been available.

Well, in our age we know. Henry Ford gave us automobiles. But what would that have meant without roads? Curtiss and Douglas and Boeing built us airliners. But how would they have gotten off the ground without runways? And what about dams and mines and canals?

Never has man built on a grander scale than in our time.

It seems an exaggeration to say that it could not have been done without the products of Holt and Best. Of course, it would have been done. Man had to build. Someone was bound to come up with the right tools. When Benjamin Holt showed his first Caterpillar in 1904, he could not have known the future of the company he started and the product he built. It was a strong company. It was a strong product. His was the right tool.

But let us not get carried away by such grand scales. Let us think small. Let us enter the mind of a child.

The time is 1948. The place is Sweden. (Well, the place is a pile of dirt in a backyard in Sweden.) He is nine years old. Yesterday he spent a long time watching a huge yellow machine they call a Caterpillar tear down the old school building in the village.

He has seen heavy wires wrapped around the brick walls, seen the wires winched home by the machine, seen the walls come tumbling down in a dust cloud, seen the machine push the rubble into mountains that could be loaded on trucks and hauled away.

He has watched the machine roll, back and forth; the huge shiny blade move, up and down; the operator pull the levers, in and out; the smoke billow from the exhaust stack, up and away. He has listened to the growling from the engine and the clanking and the creaking from the tracks.

Today, in the backyard, he has built himself something that looks like a miniature Caterpillar. He has fashioned a body from a piece of two-by-four. He has made wheels from roller-skate rollers. The tracks are sections of a bicycle inner tube, wrapped around the rollers. The blade is a piece of wooden molding. It is a crude toy. But he can move it. He can make the sounds. His imagination does the rest.

Tomorrow he will paint it yellow.

That boy was me. I never became a Caterpillar operator, but I did get to photograph them.

But what about the boy who grew up on a farm in California? His father owned many Caterpillars — the real thing. The boy started driving them when he was seven. He never needed the toy. He had the real thing.

When he became a man, it was his job to operate Caterpillars, on the farm and in his earth-moving business. But was it just a job to him? Was the machine just a machine? Or did the machine become something more than a machine? Ask him. He collects them. Has forty or fifty.

And what about the boy from Oregon? He operates a D10 now. The biggest of them all. He runs it during the third shift in a quarry in Northern California. He works the yellow giant high up on the hill. He rips the rock out of its foundations and pushes it to the edge of the hill and on down. Is it just a machine to him? Why then, at the end of a grueling work day, does he still grin when he runs his Cat straight down that hill?

What is it about this machine? Why the fascination? Is it some kind of extension of power? Is it the exhilaration of dominating the giant? Of making it roll, swing, push, rip? And the old ones; is it nostalgia? Is it the intrigue of making things come alive, run, work?

Well, let us leave it something of a mystery. Let us be content with the fact that they are what they are — old, worn, rusty, dirty, new, yellow, big, heavy, huge, gigantic, useful, efficient, kind of neat, fun to watch, fun to operate, exciting, just a machine, just a tool to get the job done . . . and a damn nuisance when they will not start.

This photograph shows only a small portion — the powerplant, actually — of the Caterpillar factory in East Peoria, Illinois. It is the site of the "mother plant" and covers a total area of 656 acres, including 190 acres under roof. As many as 19,000 employees work here.

Chapter One
Two Makes Twice as Strong

In 1883, the Holt Brothers, originally from New England, began building wagon wheels in Stockton, California. In 1886, the firm expanded the line to include combines. These monstrous machines were at first horse drawn — often by as many as forty animals. In 1890, Holt replaced the horses with steam traction engines. Then, in 1904, a track-type tractor was developed — the first to be marketed under the Caterpillar name.

In 1880, Daniel Best, a farmboy from Iowa and a frustrated prospector, invented a machine that could clean grain in the field. In 1886, expansion forced him to move from Oakland, California, to nearby San Leandro, where he was able to buy a larger facility. Best built combines already in 1885, and in 1889, introduced steam power. In 1908, he sold his company to Holt. But in 1910, Best's son began marketing his own version of the track-type tractor. This carried the Tracklayer trademark.

The next decade saw the universal acceptance of the crawler tractor. This was not in the least hurt by its application in tank warfare. It all resulted in a phenomenal growth of the Holt and Best companies, and a competition so fierce that both organizations suffered. In 1925, it was felt the two should merge. The name Caterpillar was chosen for the new organization.

A low-level shot of the Best Sixty, with its tiller steering and ample seat. Actually, it should be referred to as a sofa. The comfort factor was certainly a sales point — a long day in the field took its toll.

When Holt and Best merged in 1925, five models were chosen from the combined line. Three came from Holt. The 2-Ton and the 5-Ton are shown here. The third was the 10-Ton, which was dropped virtually right away. The 5-Ton lasted one year. The 2-Ton stayed until 1928. The 5-Ton featured to the left is part of the collection at the Bright's Livestock Ranch, Le Grand, California. The 2-Ton was found on the Porter Ranch, Salinas, California.

Next page
Here is another 2-Ton, also from the Porter Ranch. This is an example of a product from the merged organization. Notice that the Caterpillar logo now crowns the front of the radiator, while the model designation runs down its side. Just about the only item unaffected by the rust is the magneto.

The Thirty was the smallest of the two products taken from the Best range. The 1929 example, to the left, spent its working life in the California gold rush country, but is now retired — except for an occasional show appearance — at the Porter Ranch. It has been repainted and had the bearings tightened, says Porter, but otherwise nothing has been touched. The model is a wide-gauge version, especially designed for operation on steep hillsides. Notice that in this photograph the ground is sharp, while the machine is fuzzy — visual proof that this veteran is still healthy and running. The Thirty pictured above, found on the Morgantine Ranch, Greenfield, California, is in a more curious state. At some point it has apparently received a coat of white paint.

Next page
Here is collector Ed Porter at the controls of the Thirty his father bought in 1930. It has been on the ranch ever since, and is still used for post drilling. But its greatest distinction to Porter is that it was the machine he was taught to operate at the age of seven.

Pictured to the left is a Sixty, the second product from Best, and the largest in the combined line-up. It was probably also the most successful track-type tractor of the first generation. Best began producing these machines in 1919. The model lasted until 1931. This machine is part of a three-unit display at Agristruction, Selma, California. It is an extremely well preserved example of an early year, with its typical corrugated steel roof. Pictured above is a curious example. It is either a Sixty fitted with a diesel engine, or a diesel model with a Sixty radiator. In any case, it shows the type of enclosed cabin offered in the late twenties.

Next page
Here is a magnificent monument to that long-lived workhorse of Caterpillar's first generation, the Sixty. Just about the only spot where there is a bit of yellow paint left is on the top portion of the radiator, where the raised Caterpillar logo also can be seen. It, too — after sixty years — still shows some of its coat of black paint.

Chapter Two
New Models for New Growth

The first task for the new Caterpillar Tractor Company was the consolidation of the two dealer organizations. The competing networks built up by Best and Holt over the years, were of approximately equal proportions. In the end, a list of about ninety dealers was arrived at.

The second task was the creation of a new line of tractors. The company spent large sums on this effort. The first result was seen in 1927. Further models were introduced in 1928 and in 1929. Another event that would have great importance for the Caterpillar's use in road building was the 1928 acquisition of the Russel Grader Company of Minneapolis.

Already in 1909, the Holt company had set up manufacturing in East Peoria, Illinois. By 1916, production at this facility averaged fifty tractors per month. By 1918, it had doubled. Then, in connection with the merger, all tractor manufacture was concentrated to East Peoria. By 1929, the facilities consisted of twenty-five acres under roof. The work force was 4,000.

The sales figures demonstrate even more graphically the enormous expansion that took place during the four first years after the merger. The first year, 1925, saw sales of $21 million. In 1929, the figure had more than doubled, to $52 million. The future looked bright.

The Ten, introduced in 1928, was the second new product to spring from the development efforts of the merged Caterpillar organization. The drawbar output was 15 horsepower. It was the smallest of the line, and lasted until 1933.

This Ten, complete with engine covers, is an orchard version. The low position of the seat allowed better clearance for the operator as he maneuvered below the tree branches. Ed Porter is at the controls of a machine he picked up in Watsonville, California, where it has been used in an apple orchard. The lever on the left is the hand-operated clutch. The two other levers control the speed of the tracks — pulling back on the left lever results in a left turn, while pulling back on the right results in a right turn. The brakes are foot operated. The round-knobbed lever in the middle is the gearshift — three forward gears and one reverse. The throttle lever is obscured in this picture, but is operated with the right hand. Only one gauge was deemed necessary in those days — that of the oil pressure.

Next page
This is a Ten manufactured toward the end of the production run. It is also part of the Porter collection. Notice the elaborate air-cleaner unit, with its quaint glass jar where the impurities are collected.

Pictured to the left — in retirement on the Porter Ranch — is a poppy-surrounded Fifteen. This model was introduced in 1919, and stayed in the catalog until 1933. The output was 22 horsepower, measured at the drawbar. Pictured above is another Porter Ranch survivor, a Twenty. This model was the first introduced after the merger, and arrived in 1927. The version shown here, as is clearly visible in the picture, is powered by the flathead Cat engine. It was listed as producing 23 horsepower at the drawbar. The final curtain for this model also came in 1933.

Next page
Another Twenty, this one with a roof over its head. The location is a barn on the Morgantine Ranch. This picture shows the flathead engine from the other side, exposing its decoratively curving exhaust manifold.

The Twenty-Two appeared in 1934, and lasted until 1939. The drawbar output was 25 horsepower. At this point the old Caterpillar logo, with its undulating script, had been replaced by one using a crisp no-nonsense face. Also, it was no longer found at the top of the radiator — the model designation now occupied this spot — but down its side. This well-preserved example is part of the large Bright collection in Le Grand, California.

The models featured in this spread, both reclining in the Porter Ranch backyard, are quite unusual. The Twenty-Five, to the left, was only available for two years. It was introduced in 1931 and discontinued in 1933. The Twenty-Eight, above, took over that year, but it also lasted only two years. Drawbar output was 25 and 28 horsepower, respectively.

The Thirty-Five — also in the Porter collection — is another short-lived model, lasting only from 1932 until 1934. Thirty-eight horses were available at the drawbar. Notice that the Caterpillar logo is again located at the top of the radiator. The organization of all the models, their production years and numbers, their variances and so on, gathered into a printed volume would be a major task, and would result in a brick of a book.

Next page
The Porter Ranch also contains this unique survivor. The unusual part is not so much the Fifty — in production between 1931 and 1937 — but the bulldozing equipment that almost hides the Cat. Manufactured by R. G. Torneau, it represents the type used in those early days. The ensemble was rescued from a junkyard in Watsonville, California. In this context, a few words on prices: They vary from $50 to $300 and up to $500 for the rusty old derelicts, depending on model. For a running example with some paint still left, the prices vary from, say, $600 up to $1,000, also dependent on model. For choice collector pieces, such as an old Sixty, prices can go as high as $10,000 for a pristine example.

Chapter Three
Survival of the Fittest

When the stock market came crashing down in 1929, it at first did not seem to have a great impact on Caterpillar. Sales in 1930 dropped only about ten percent. Much of this was the result of contracts with the Soviet Union. One single order was for as many as 1,350 Cat Sixties. This was symptomatic of the company's future interaction on a global level — Caterpillar helped develop Russian agriculture, while Russia helped save Caterpillar.

In 1922, 166 companies had been engaged in tractor manufacture — a majority of these were building non-crawlers. By 1933, the number was down to twenty. Caterpillar had also been affected. In 1932, sales dropped to $13 million. It was the first year of no profit. In 1933, salaries were cut twenty percent, and the work week reduced to four days.

The way out of the slump came as a result of the consistent policy of investing in research and development. Both Best and Holt had experimented with diesel engines long before the merger, but it took their combined resources to bring the efforts to fruition.

Caterpillar's Diesel Sixty was introduced in 1931. Thanks to thorough testing, it was not only supremely dependable, but cut the cost of operating in half, as a result of its superior fuel economy.

Up until the early thirties, the power sources of the Caterpillar tractors were always gasoline engines. After 1936 — the year the Forty was eliminated from the sales catalog — virtually all models had diesel engines. This meant a new look to the engine compartment, as seen here on an RD7.

These pictures truly transport the viewer back to the thirties, thanks to Ed Porter's skillful modeling. This machine, the Diesel Thirty-Five — in production between 1933 and 1934 — was one of the pioneer diesels. It put out 40 horsepower at the drawbar. The first to arrive was the Diesel Sixty, which was introduced in 1931. Its drawbar output was 70 horsepower.

Here is a Diesel Forty from the Porter Ranch. It was produced between 1934 and 1936, and is considered one of the more rare models. It was powered by a three-cylinder diesel. The output was 44 horsepower at the drawbar.

The RD7, seen here in a Porter Ranch shed from an appropriate era, was a very popular model. No less than 10,000 units were made. Its forerunner was the Diesel Fifty, built between 1933 and 1936. The RD7 lasted until 1941, when it, with necessary improvements, became the D7 — a model of World War II fame. Caterpillar's D-designation became synonymous with the yellow machines, and is still used today to denote the various models.

46

Chapter Four
Tracks Across the Fields

The need for the track-type tractor in agriculture was actually what sparked its creation. Stockton, where Benjamin Holt had chosen to set up his company, is located right on the edge of the vast flat-lands of California's San Joaquin Valley. To the west lies the Sacramento River delta. The utilization of this water for the irrigation of the valley, triggered a boom that rivaled that of the gold rush.

The vastness of the farms that were formed as a result of this great settling of the land — one, for example, consisted of as much as 36,000 acres — made mechanization a must. And the curious characteristics of the deep, rich and spongy soil — when dry, so volatile that a spark could ignite a smoldering underground blaze; when wet, so treacherous men and horses and machinery could be swallowed — made the track-type tractor a natural choice.

An ad from the early years of the century extolls the virtues of the Caterpillar, "so named on account of the appearance of its traction mechanism while in motion": "Does not pack the soil; will run as well on soft boggy soil as on hard land, and can ride with facility over the most undulating ground." To this day, Caterpillar yellow is the dominating color of the machines working the fields in this part of the farming world.

A most popular machine for small and medium size farms, was the D4, introduced in 1936. It weighed 9,400 pounds. Output at the drawbar was 41 horsepower. Here, a 1948 vintage is patrolling an orchard.

This little D2 was found in a small valley on the
Central California coast, not far from Avila Beach.
Nearing the age of fifty, it is still going strong. A most
versatile machine, the D2 is a real farming classic.
The drawbar power is 31 horsepower.

Next page
This D4, found on a farm near Santa Paula, California,
has had a lot of hard use. As can be seen, various
implement attachments have become permanent,
but this in no way distracts from the workhorse look
of this old-timer.

Pictured here is an often-occurring scene when preparing an old diesel Cat for action. The operator must first start a small single-cylinder gasoline engine. This is in turn used to crank up the main engine. Here a D4 is playing hard to get, blowing a cloud of blue smoke in the operator's face.

Next page
Don Waters, a walnut farmer in Sutter County, California, rides his dependable old D4 — the special low-seat orchard version. It came with the farm, and was bought by the original owner in 1946, Waters says. The engine has been overhauled only once in all these years.

This photograph speaks eloquently of the hardships as well as the pleasures facing the operator of a Caterpillar on the farm — the dust, the scorching sun, the wide-open spaces, the blue-faded mountains in the distance. Missing from the picture — showing a D5 in Salinas Valley, California — are only the sounds from the engine and the tracks.

Next page
Here a D6 is at work near Greenfield, California. It pulls a land plane. This piece of equipment is hydraulically operated, and some of these giants can reach a length of 100 feet. The fact that the field is level is important for proper irrigation.

A classic view of the Caterpillar operator at work. The seemingly monotonous task is in fact quite demanding. The methodical advance across the field requires constant monitoring and correction of the direction.

Next page
This is how a D6, based in a farm community east of Stockton, California, is transported. The bed tips up for easy roll-back of the Cat. The implement is a special type of plow used to produce the deep irrigation ditches that surround the fields.

The endless fields of the country east of Paso Robles, California, with their gently rolling hills, is the perfect playground for these big D8H Cats from the early seventies. The six-cylinder engines produce close to 300 horsepower at the drawbar. Notice the flag in the picture above, carried to warn fellow operators on the other side of the hill.

Seen in this photograph is the luxuriously equipped, air-conditioned "office" of one of the D8H machines pictured on the previous page.

Next page
Caterpillar produces a line of five track-type loaders. Seen here is the smallest, the 931B. It fits the bill perfectly for the type of work it performs — loading boxes of just-harvested celery on the fertile fields near Camarillo, California.

Chapter Five
Moving Earth on a Large Scale

Ever since, in 1908, the engineers of the 230-mile-long Los Angeles Aqueduct decided to use Caterpillar tractors for their large-scale earth-moving operations — giving Benjamin Holt invaluable publicity as well as incentive to gear up for mass production — this type of activity has become synonymous with the big yellow machines.

Surprisingly early on, the Caterpillar tractor reached beyond the borders of region and country, beginning the tradition of worldwide involvement. Mexico was first, then came Argentina and Canada. The virtues of the Caterpillar soon spread its use to Europe and North Africa, and later to every corner of the world.

The Caterpillar was one of the heroes of World War II — certainly not referred to in as lofty terms as the Mustangs and the Shermans, but still heroes. The Caterpillar was often the first to go ashore during amphibious assaults, and its role in building airfields and roads was one of major importance for the success of the war effort.

After the war, the demand for earth-moving equipment resulted in the development of new products — not only tractors -but scrapers, wagons, bulldozers, blades and rippers.

Even though the presence of the Caterpillar in farming is well known, it is its use in earth moving that has made the greatest impact, especially where the big machines are concerned. Here a D10 is bringing a load of dirt to another Caterpillar product, a wheel loader.

A D5B on a construction site in California. This 23,300 pound unit is produced at the Caterpillar factory in Grenoble, France. It has a drawbar output, depending on gearing, of between 92 and 136 horsepower. The smallest model in the recent line-up is the 14,700 pound D3B. This, and the next size up — the 16,700 pound D4E — are both built in the Caterpillar/Mitsubishi facilities in Sagamihara, Japan. The 29,000 pound D6D is built in Glasgow, Scotland.

Next page
An old D6 has been left to the elements — temporarily, one suspects. Incredibly, ten years from now not much will have changed, except for the seat cushions, and the engine may very well start on the first or second try. The setting, an orchard along the road to Fillmore, California, provides both avocados and oranges for the enjoyment of the resting workhorse.

An aging D7 still performs its earth-moving duties adequately in a quarry near Flagstaff, Arizona. A closer look reveals a criss-cross pattern on the face of the blade. This is referred to as hard-facing. The theory is that it helps prevent wear — dirt will collect in the spaces between the welds, causing dirt to wear against dirt.

Next page
The silhouette of an American classic. This is the D8H — late fifties vintage. Operator John McCarroll lifts the blade and retraces his path, rolling slowly on top of a levee along the Mississippi River.

John McCarroll of Moline, Illinois, has operated a variety of old Cats during his thirty years at the controls. Here he is captured with the D8H that has been his companion for the past three years. "This guy doesn't need a break, but I do," McCarroll says, and opens his lunch box. "How much did the Cat cost new? Well, back in the late fifties, we used to figure a dollar a pound — 54,000 pounds — 54,000 dollars."

Next page
Jim Reeves, another veteran Cat operator, builds a lagoon on a dairy farm in Escalon, California. He alternates between ripping, as in the picture, and bull-dozing. Later in the day, when he will have reached the called-for depth of 12 feet, only the exhaust plume will give him away to a casual passer-by.

This photograph, from a quarry along the shore of the East San Francisco Bay, shows a D8K — the next-to-newest generation of the big Cats — involved in a slightly delicate maneuver. The operator must move the Cat up to the top of the sand mountain, advance slowly until a slide is triggered, then retreat quickly, before the avalanche of sand reaches the machine. No sweat.

A D8K at work on a construction site along Interstate 5, north of the Los Angeles Basin. Here it performs one of the multitude of tasks at which it is adept. This piece of equipment is referred to as a sheep's-foot roller, and is used for compacting the ground.

Next page
No dump site is complete without a Cat. This D8K is employed in Mountain View, California. Moving like a ship in heavy seas, sinking, rising, rolling, the dozer blade — with an extension — is pushing its own wave of trash.

The Cats engaged in this job — based at the
Madonna Construction Company in San Luis Obispo
— are no strangers to the area south of Big Sur on
the California Coast. Every year, it seems, there is a
big slide, completely cutting off traffic on Highway 1,
a major tourist route. So the Cats have to move in.
And they have to work from daybreak to dusk. Still,
it will take months before the mountain of dirt is
gone. For the operators, a view of the Pacific comes
with the job.

For nearly two decades — from its introduction in 1959, to the introduction in 1977 of the D10 — the D9 was the biggest Cat around. In this photograph from California's Highway 1 slide area, the big machine looks like a small toy against the backdrop of the mountain.

These pictures show further scenes from working the big slide on the California Coast. Just before the arrival of dusk, the operators are walkie-talkied down from their perch at the top of the slide. To the left, the big D9G has just been refueled. To the right, its swing-shaft bearings receive a couple of shots of grease.

Here is the big Ten! All two stories of it — all 174,000
pounds of it. A photograph really does not do it
justice. The machine must be seen. This can be hard
to do, since these giants are seldom operating
outside their habitats of quarries and mines.
Something of the size can be appreciated by
comparing it to operator Troy Johnson, pictured
above, as he descends from his throne.

The D10 is powered by Caterpillar's D348 engine. A
V-12, it has a displacement of 1,786 cubic inches, and
a flywheel rating of 700 horsepower at 1,800
revolutions per minute. The machine stands almost
15 feet high. The fuel tank holds 383 gallons.
Extraordinary measurements for an extraordinary
machine. To the right, as the sun sets, operator Troy
Johnson prepares for his descent to base.

These pictures from a construction site in Santa Monica, California, show the D10 performing one of its premier functions — ripping. This eliminates the old method of drilling and blasting. The special bogie roller-type undercarriage is one of its big assets. It means a maximum of traction. Traction, weight, horsepower — the keys to effective ripping. This heavyweight belongs to David T. Price, Inc., of Escalon, California. Oscar Carlsen is at the controls.

Time for a major overhaul. David T. Price, Inc. — located east of Modesto, California — bought this machine in 1980. It has since run about 12,000 hours. The company has its own skilled mechanics perform this maintenance. In the picture, the track assembly — a ten-ton chunk of iron — is being removed. The pivot shaft is exposed just to the left of the ladder. The engine will also get its share of attention, with the rod and main bearings being changed. "Besides being used on construction sites all over California, this machine is probably the only D10 engaged in agricultural tasks as well," says Price. "The soil around here is such that it needs ripping. And for the big field — sometimes 2,000 acres — we run this big D10 with the big eight-foot shank."

Chapter Six
A New Generation of Giants

The sixties catapulted the Caterpillar company into the realm of the world's major industrial organizations. An economic boom of never-before-seen dimensions, required tens of thousands of miles of new highways. The emergence of the jet airliner meant new and larger airports. Multiplying energy needs demanded the construction of dams and mines.

In the late sixties, Caterpillar embarked on yet another ambitious development program, which resulted in the 1974 introduction of a new and complete line of diesel engines. These were intended for all possible applications, such as marine and industrial uses, for truck and generator purposes, and for Caterpillar's own growing product line.

In 1977, a new track-type tractor was introduced. Its designation was D10. It was the largest and most advanced ever constructed. The most distinctive characteristic was the elevated drive sprocket. This design meant a prolonged lifespan for the powertrain. Later the D7, the D8 and the D9 were redesigned according to the same principle.

In 1986, an even larger machine was introduced, the D11. Heavier, stronger and with longer tracks, this tractor — the giant of the giants — is a further manifestation of Caterpillar's leadership in the industry.

A low-level angle of the Caterpillar D11N accentuates the formidable size of this, the largest and the newest in the product line-up — so new, in fact, was the model that this photograph probably was the first not taken for the company's own publicity. The D11N was officially introduced on May 1, 1986.

Previous page
A D11N receiving the final touches inside the Caterpillar tractor plant in Peoria, Illinois. This facility, which produces the 7, 8, 9, 10 and 11 models, was completed in 1977, and was at that time one of the world's most modern assembly plants. It still is a model of advanced efficiency and spotless appearance.

In this picture a D11N has reached the stage where it is moved outside in the lot. It shows clearly one of the obvious tell-tale signs of the new model, the greater angle of the rear portion of the tracks from the sprocket on down. The D11N is longer, placing twenty-one inches more track on the ground, which of course increases traction.

The D11N is bigger all around than the D10 it replaces. The flywheel power is up ten percent to 770 horsepower, the weight is up 5.5 percent to 204,500 pounds, the peak torque is up, the weight-to-power ratio is up, the ground clearance is up, and so on — all improving the efficiency of the new machine. The picture above features the impressive ripper. With its shank lifted, it looks like a giant stinger.

A scene from the backyard of the Caterpillar tractor plant, where row after row of machines, in various stages of completion, cover acre after acre. During a rain storm, as in this photograph, it was an eerie experience to walk along these rows of giants, especially since they all seemed alive — at this stage of the testing procedure they all have their engines running.

Chapter Seven
Old Cats Never Die

The Caterpillar organization enters the new era with a new name. Caterpillar Tractor Company has now become Caterpillar Inc. This reflects the company's diversified product line. Both "Caterpillar Inc." and "Cat," as well as the "C," are registered trademarks.

The early eighties — with a decline of large construction projects, record-high interest rates, currency imbalances, just to mention some of the multitude of problems that faced a company such as Caterpillar — meant a drastic trimming of the operations.

In 1982, for the first time in fifty years, the company lost money. Also for the first time in fifty years, Caterpillar, in 1983, was forced to close plants and lay off workers. From a peak of 90,000 employees, the Caterpillar company now employs 54,000 worldwide. With all its operations streamlined and lean, the future once again looks bright.

But the old Caterpillars of fields and barns across the nation and the world, know nothing of these problems; they could care less. For them, life is good. Some of them are still working once in a while. But most of them are just sitting there, resting, enjoying the scenery — and the attention of some nostalgia-nut admirer. These old Cats never die . . .

This is the Porter Ranch, nestled in the foothills to the east of Salinas, California. Salinas is Steinbeck country, the town where he grew up, and the inspiration for his famous novel, East of Eden. Well, if east of Eden meant next to Paradise, these old Cats have come to rest in the right place.

No part of a Caterpillar is ever left to waste. In equipment yards all over the country, and the world — the photograph on this and the following pages were taken at Ray Newman's Tractorland in Riverside, California — one will encounter scenes like these. The tracks to the left can be resurrected at any time. Rust means nothing. And the old wheel above, might be picked up by a collector tomorrow.

In these photographs, the massive engine blocks, the snaking manifolds, the curling tubes and lines, once hot from combustion, once channeling rushing gasses, once pumping oils and fuels, have now taken on a different dimension — decorative sculptures of color and form — charming mementos from a nostalgic past.

Although Caterpillar engines seem to run forever, it sometimes happens that they reach the end of the road. This unit must have given its operator a most unfriendly treatment. And it must have gotten some unfriendly phrases in return, no doubt. It looks as if a thrown rod might have been the problem. No good for an overhaul now, but good for parts.

Next page
Curiously vulnerable they seem, these pistons. Out of their cozy, well-oiled environment, they face the heartless cruelty of the elements. All they can do now is wait for the moment when they will be saved and put to good use again.

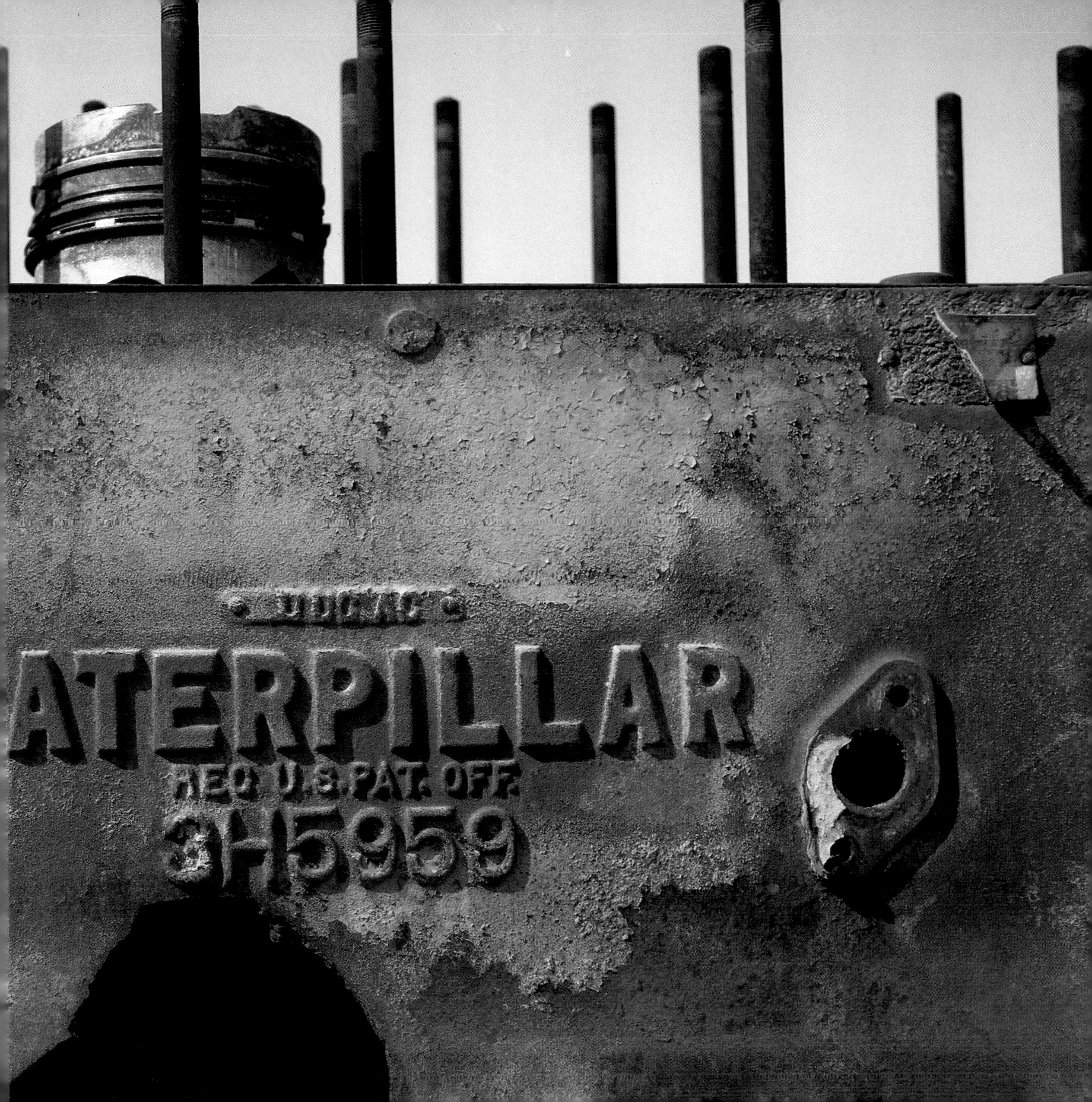
ATERPILLAR
REG U.S. PAT. OFF.
3H5959

Here is another part from the deep insides of the
Caterpillar engine — a crankshaft. Even in this
condition it can be de-blasted, re-welded and ground
back to the original specifications. And this
procedure may be cheaper than buying new. Just to
take the ultimate example, the crankshaft for a V-12
engine costs close to $9,000.

Here is an old Holt 5-ton from the early twenties running at full speed, still going strong after all these years -a tribute to the longevity of the machines Benjamin Holt built.